GRAPHIC AMERICA

TAMING THE WEST

DARREN SECHRIST

Crabtree Publishing Company
www.crabtreebooks.com

Crabtree Publishing Company
www.crabtreebooks.com

Author:
Darren Sechrist
Coordinating editor:
Chester Fisher
Editors:
Scholastic Ventures Inc.
Molly Aloian
Copy editor:
Scholastic Ventures Inc.
Proofreaders:
Adrianna Morganelli
Crystal Sikkens
Project editor:
Robert Walker
Production coordinator:
Katherine Berti

Prepress technicians:
Ken Wright
Katherine Kantor
Logo design:
Samantha Crabtree
Project manager:
Santosh Vasudevan (Q2AMedia)
Art direction:
Rahul Dhiman (Q2AMedia)
Design:
Shweta Niga (Q2AMedia)
Illustrations:
Q2AMedia

Library and Archives Canada Cataloguing in Publication

Sechrist, Darren
Taming the West / Darren Sechrist.

(Graphic America)
Includes index.
ISBN 978-0-7787-4188-6 (bound).--ISBN 978-0-7787-4215-9 (pbk.)

1. Frontier and pioneer life--West (U.S.)--Comic books, strips, etc.--Juvenile literature. 2. West (U.S.)--History--19th century--Comic books, strips, etc.--Juvenile literature. 3. West (U.S.)--Biography--Comic

books, strips, etc.--Juvenile literature. I. Title. II. Series.

F596.S42 2008 j978'.02 C2008-906280-9

Library of Congress Cataloging-in-Publication Data

Sechrist, Darren.
Taming the West / Darren Sechrist.
p. cm. -- (Graphic America)
Includes index.
ISBN-13: 978-0-7787-4215-9 (pbk. : alk. paper)
ISBN-10: 0-7787-4215-6 (pbk. : alk. paper)
ISBN-13: 978-0-7787-4188-6 (reinforced library binding : alk. paper)
ISBN-10: 0-7787-4188-5 (reinforced library binding : alk. paper)
1. Frontier and pioneer life--West (U.S.)--Comic books, strips, etc.--Juvenile literature. 2. West (U.S.)--History--Comic books, strips, etc.--Juvenile literature. 3. West (U.S.)--Biography--Comic books, strips, etc.--Juvenile literature. 4. Graphic novels. I. Title. II. Series.

F596.S325 2009
978'.02--dc22

2008041854

Crabtree Publishing Company
www.crabtreebooks.com 1-800-387-7650

Printed in the USA/092017/JF20170802

Published in Canada
Crabtree Publishing
616 Welland Ave.
St. Catharines, ON
L2M 5V6

Published in the United States
Crabtree Publishing
PMB59051
350 Fifth Ave., 59th Floor
New York, NY 10118

Published in the United Kingdom
Crabtree Publishing
Maritime House
Basin Road North, Hove
BN41 1WR

Published in Australia
Crabtree Publishing
3 Charles Street
Coburg North
VIC, 3058

CONTENTS

EARLY MEETINGS WITH THE NATIVE AMERICANS

WE HAVE MUCH TO LEARN FROM YOU ABOUT THIS WONDERFUL LAND.

*IN THE MID-1800S, THE YOUNG NATION OF THE **UNITED** STATES GREW QUICKLY TO SPREAD TO THE WESTERN PART OF NORTH AMERICA. ONE MAJOR ISSUE WAS HOW TO LIVE WITH THE **NATIVE AMERICANS** WHO WERE ALREADY THERE. THIS SITUATION STARTED IN EASTERN NORTH AMERICA WHEN COLUMBUS ARRIVED IN 1492. FOR HUNDREDS OF YEARS, WHITE **SETTLERS** AND NATIVE AMERICANS HAD TO FIND WAYS TO LIVE SIDE BY SIDE.*

*THOUGH THERE WERE SOME TIMES OF PEACE BETWEEN THE TWO GROUPS, FIGHTING WAS MORE COMMON. AN EARLY WHITE COLONY AT JAMESTOWN FOUGHT A BITTER BATTLE AGAINST THE NATIVE AMERICANS IN THE 1600S. THE GROWING DEMANDS OF THE COLONY HAD CAUSED THE ALGONKIAN NATION TO ATTACK. THE **COLONISTS** FOUGHT BACK. THEY BURNED DOWN THEIR CORN CROPS AND DESTROYED THEIR HOMES.*

BURN THEM ALL—EVERY LAST ONE!

WE CAN COME THROUGH THE WOODS ON THIS PATH AND ATTACK THE FORCE FROM THE EAST.
WE'LL TAKE THEM BY SURPRISE!
WARS WITH THE NATIVE AMERICANS FOLLOWED AS THE BRITISH SETTLED ALONG THE EAST COAST. THE NATIVE AMERICANS WERE EVEN INVOLVED IN BATTLES BETWEEN THE FRENCH AND BRITISH IN NORTH AMERICA. THESE FOUR WARS, HELD BETWEEN 1689 AND 1763, BECAME KNOWN AS THE FRENCH AND INDIAN WARS. DIFFERENT NATIONS FOUGHT ON EACH SIDE.

THE BRITISH DEFEATED THE FRENCH, BUT THIS DID NOT END CONFLICTS WITH THE NATIVE AMERICANS. THE START OF THE REVOLUTIONARY WAR IN 1775 MADE MATTERS WORSE. MOST NATIONS HELPED THE BRITISH AGAINST THE COLONISTS. THIS CREATED DISTRUST WITH THE COLONISTS. THAT HURT THE CHANCES FOR PEACE FOR YEARS TO COME.

THE LAND UP TO THE RIVER WILL BE YOURS. BUT THAT IS AS FAR AS WE WILL ALLOW.
YES, IT IS AGREED.
WE WILL SEE ABOUT THAT.
THE AGREEMENT THAT ENDED THE REVOLUTIONARY WAR SET THE BORDERS OF THE UNITED STATES. BUT IT ALSO LEFT OUT THE LAND RIGHTS OF THE NATIVE AMERICANS. THE NEW NATION KEPT GROWING TO THE WEST. SOMETIMES ITS LEADERS RESPECTED THE NATIVE AMERICANS' RIGHT TO THEIR HOMELANDS, BUT MOST TIMES LAND WAS TAKEN BY FORCE.

WILL WE LET OURSELVES BE DESTROYED IN OUR TURN WITHOUT A STRUGGLE, GIVE UP OUR HOMES, OUR COUNTRY **BEQUEATHED** TO US BY THE GREAT SPIRIT, THE GRAVES OF OUR DEAD AND EVERYTHING THAT IS DEAR AND SACRED TO US? I KNOW YOU WILL CRY WITH ME, 'NEVER! NEVER!' *
THE MANY NATIONS OF NORTH AMERICA HAD LITTLE SUCCESS FIGHTING U.S. FORCES ON THEIR OWN. BUT IN THE EARLY 1800S, A GREAT SHAWNEE LEADER NAMED TECUMSEH BEGAN TO BRING TOGETHER THE NATIONS IN OHIO. HE TOLD THEM THEY SHOULD NOT SELL ANY MORE LAND TO THE AMERICANS.

*ACTUAL QUOTE

IN 1811, THE SHAWNEE BATTLED WITH U.S. SOLDIERS WHILE TECUMSEH WAS TRAVELING TO GET OTHER NATIONS TO JOIN HIM. THEIR VILLAGE WAS DESTROYED IN THE BATTLE OF TIPPECANOE, BUT TECUMSEH HAD SURVIVED.
TECUMSEH, SPEAK TO ME.
WE HAVE LOST OUR LEADER!
TECUMSEH WENT ON TO HELP THE BRITISH AGAINST THE AMERICANS IN THE WAR OF 1812. HE SERVED AS A **GENERAL** AND LED MORE THAN 2,000 MEN. OTHER NATIVE AMERICANS HELPED THE BRITISH, TOO. TECUMSEH DIED DURING A BATTLE IN 1813. A TREATY ENDED THE WAR IN 1815. EARLY NATIVE AMERICAN **RESISTANCE** IN THE EAST HAD COME TO AN END.

THE INDIAN WARS

THESE TREATIES, BEING PROBABLY THE LAST WHICH WILL EVER BE MADE WITH THEM, ARE CHARACTERIZED BY GREAT LIBERALITY ON THE PART OF THE GOVERNMENT. THEY GIVE THE INDIANS A LIBERAL SUM IN CONSIDERATION OF THEIR REMOVAL, AND COMFORTABLE **SUBSISTENCE** ON THEIR ARRIVAL AT THEIR NEW HOMES.*
IN 1830, U.S. PRESIDENT ANDREW JACKSON SIGNED THE INDIAN REMOVAL ACT INTO LAW. IT SAID THAT ALL NATIVE AMERICANS MUST BE MOVED WEST OF THE MISSISSIPPI RIVER. NATIVE AMERICAN NATIONS WERE PAID VERY SMALL AMOUNTS FOR THEIR LOSS OF LAND.

YOU NEED TO KEEP MOVING, OR ELSE.
ONE FAMOUS EXAMPLE OF NATIVE AMERICAN REMOVAL WAS THE "TRAIL OF TEARS." AROUND 15,000 CHEROKEE WERE REMOVED FROM THEIR HOMES IN GEORGIA. U.S. SOLDIERS THEN MARCHED THEM FOR MONTHS, TO OKLAHOMA. FOOD AND WATER WERE HARD TO FIND. MORE THAN 4,000 CHEROKEE DIED ON THE TRIP.
I CANNOT GO ANY FURTHER.

THE U.S. GOVERNMENT MOVED NATION AFTER NATION OF NATIVE AMERICANS AWAY FROM THEIR LANDS. HOWEVER, A FEW FOUGHT BACK. A CHIEF NAMED BLACK HAWK LED THE SAUK AND FOX NATIONS TO RISE UP AGAINST U.S. SOLDIERS. THE SEMINOLE NATION OF FLORIDA RESISTED, TOO. BOTH WERE DEFEATED AND REMOVED TO THE WEST ANYWAY.

THESE MEN CANNOT BE TRUSTED. THEY AIM TO TAKE OUR LANDS WITH A SWEEP OF THE PEN. WE SHALL NOT ALLOW IT!

THE UNITED STATES GREW FURTHER WEST BY TAKING CONTROL OF TEXAS AND WINNING THE MEXICAN AMERICAN WAR. THE DISCOVERY OF GOLD IN CALIFORNIA AND THE GOOD FARMING LANDS IN OREGON DREW MORE AMERICANS TO MOVE WEST. MORE FIGHTING WITH NATIVE AMERICANS WAS SOON TO FOLLOW.
EACH DAY, MORE WHITE MEN COME. SOON, THEY WILL BE EVERYWHERE.

RUN. RUN FOR YOUR LIFE! WE'RE UNDER ATTACK.
NATIVE AMERICANS DID NOT LIKE TO SEE WHITE SETTLERS MOVING WEST AND TAKING EVEN MORE OF THEIR LANDS, DESTROYING WILDLIFE, AND SPREADING DISEASE. NATIVE NATIONS WOULD OFTEN ATTACK AMERICAN SETTLEMENTS OR FIGHT SETTLERS ON THE TRAILS. THE AMERICAN GOVERNMENT BEGAN BUILDING **MILITARY** FORTS TO PROTECT THE SETTLERS.

I CAN'T SEE AN END TO THEM. THEY JUST KEEP COMING FROM ALL SIDES!
HOW MANY ARE THERE?
SOME OF THE LARGEST BATTLES WERE WITH THE SIOUX AND THE CHEYENNE. IN 1876, LIEUTENANT COLONEL ARMSTRONG CUSTER LED AN ATTACK ON A NATIVE AMERICAN VILLAGE ALONG THE LITTLE BIGHORN RIVER. THE SIOUX AND CHEYENNE HAD A MUCH BIGGER FORCE THAN CUSTER. THE NATIVE AMERICANS KILLED CUSTER AND HIS MEN. KNOWN AS "CUSTER'S LAST STAND," IT WAS ONE OF THE WORST DEFEATS IN U.S. HISTORY.

I WAS NO CHIEF AND NEVER HAD BEEN, BUT BECAUSE I HAD BEEN MORE DEEPLY WRONGED THAN OTHERS, THIS HONOR WAS CONFERRED UPON ME, AND I RESOLVED TO PROVE WORTHY OF THE TRUST.*
WAR RAGED IN NEW MEXICO AND ARIZONA AS WELL. IN 1875, THE APACHE NATION HAD BEEN MOVED TO NEW MEXICO. FOR THE NEXT TEN YEARS, THE APACHE WARRIOR GERONIMO ATTACKED U.S. SOLDIERS. WHEN GERONIMO FINALLY GAVE UP IN 1886, THE APACHE WERE DEFEATED.

THE WHITE MAN WILL BE GONE. THE BUFFALO THAT ONCE ROAMED THESE PLAINS WILL RETURN. AND WE WILL RULE AGAIN.
THE CAPTURE OF GERONIMO ENDED NATIVE AMERICAN FIGHTING IN THE WEST. BUT ONE TERRIBLE EVENT REMAINED. A NEW RELIGION KNOWN AS THE GHOST DANCE PROMISED A PEACEFUL WORLD WITH ONLY NATIVE AMERICANS. THE GHOST DANCING UPSET AND FRIGHTENED SOLDIERS IN SOUTH DAKOTA. THEY CALLED IN MORE TROOPS. THE SOLDIERS KILLED CHIEF SITTING BULL AND MORE THAN 150 OTHERS, INCLUDING WOMEN AND CHILDREN. THIS WAS CALLED THE WOUNDED KNEE MASSACRE.

FAMILIES ON THE FRONTIER

IN 1848, GOLD WAS DISCOVERED IN CALIFORNIA. STARTING IN 1849, MANY AMERICAN SETTLERS HEADED WEST HOPING TO GET RICH.
OTHERS, LIKE THE **MORMONS**, SAW A NEW WORLD WHERE THEY COULD PRACTICE THEIR RELIGION FREELY.
THE GOLD IN THESE STREAMS WILL MAKE US ALL RICH.

I AM LOOKING TO MOVE MY FAMILY TO MONTANA AND MAKE A NEW LIFE.
I AM HOPING TO DO IT ALONE IN THE DAKOTAS.
THE HOMESTEAD ACT OF 1862 WAS ANOTHER DRAW. IT GAVE AWAY 160 ACRES (65 HECTARES) OF LAND TO FAMILIES WILLING TO MOVE WEST. THEY HAD TO USE THE LAND AS A HOME AND A FARM. BY 1900, MORE THAN 600,000 SETTLERS HAD TAKEN ADVANTAGE OF THE OFFER.

MANY FAMILIES SPENT MONTHS TAKING THE HARD TRIP ON THE TRAILS TO THEIR NEW HOMES. ONCE THEY ARRIVED, THEY SET ABOUT BUILDING THEIR HOMES. THE EARLIEST HOUSES WERE MADE OF BRICKS OF DIRT, OR "SOD." THEY WERE CALLED **"SODDIES."** AFTER GETTING THEIR FARMS SET UP, FAMILIES HAD ENOUGH MONEY TO REPLACE THEIR SODDIES WITH WOOD-FRAMED HOUSES.

HOW SOON CAN WE REPLACE IT WITH ONE MADE OF WOOD?
IT IS BEAUTIFUL IN ITS OWN WAY, ISN'T IT?

THE WOODEN HOMES WERE NOT FANCY. THEY OFTEN STARTED OUT AS A SINGLE ROOM, WITH A DIRT FLOOR. THERE WERE FEW STORES AND MONEY WAS HARD TO EARN. FAMILIES SURVIVED BY MAKING MANY THINGS THEMSELVES. THEY GREW CROPS AND HUNTED ANIMALS FOR FOOD. CLOTHING WAS MADE BY HAND. HEAT WAS USUALLY PROVIDED BY A WOOD STOVE AND OIL LAMPS WERE USED FOR LIGHT.
THIS LOOKS LIKE A FINE MEAL. WE HAVE MUCH TO BE THANKFUL FOR. JOSEPH, YOU MAY SAY GRACE TONIGHT.
YES, FATHER. DEAR LORD...

THE LIVES OF **FRONTIER** FAMILIES WERE FILLED WITH HARD WORK. THE MEN AND BOYS SPENT THEIR DAYS IN THE FIELDS. WOMEN AND CHILDREN TOOK CARE OF COOKING, CLEANING, AND CHORES AROUND THE HOUSE.

WE WILL SOON HAVE A FINE SCHOOLHOUSE FOR OUR CHILDREN.
WHEN THEY HAD COMPLETED THEIR HOMES, FRONTIER FAMILIES PITCHED IN TO HELP BUILD THEIR TOWNS. THEY BUILT SCHOOLS, STORES, AND OTHER IMPORTANT BUILDINGS.

CHURCHES WERE GATHERING PLACES IN MANY FRONTIER TOWNS. THEY WERE OFTEN BUILT WHERE ROADS MET. THIS ALLOWED MANY PEOPLE TO ATTEND SERVICES AND BUILT A SENSE OF COMMUNITY.

WELCOME, BROTHERS AND SISTERS. LET US PRAY TOGETHER.

THE SALOON WAS ANOTHER POPULAR PLACE IN THE WEST. THESE USUALLY APPEARED IN **BOOMTOWNS** THAT WERE BUILT QUICKLY AFTER THE GOLD RUSHES. MINERS AND COWBOYS WHO WENT TO SALOONS MIGHT STOP IN FOR A DRINK OR A CARD GAME. THESE WERE ROUGH PLACES. FIGHTS OFTEN BROKE OUT.
THESE CARDS ARE MARKED. YOU'RE CHEATIN' ME, AND YOU'RE NOT TAKING NO MONEY OF MINE!

OUTLAWS OF THE OLD WEST

HARRY'S
SALOON
DRAW!
THE WEST GREW QUICKLY. TOWNS WERE BUILT OVERNIGHT, BUT THE LAW HAD TROUBLE KEEPING UP. GUNFIGHTS AND OTHER KINDS OF VIOLENCE HAPPENED OFTEN.

MANY OUTLAWS FORMED GANGS THAT STOLE CATTLE, ROBBED BANKS, AND CAUSED ALL SORTS OF TROUBLE. IN THE NEW TOWNS OF THE WEST, THERE WAS LITTLE TO STOP THEM.
HAND OVER YOUR MONEY AND YOUR JEWELRY TO ZEKE HERE. MAYBE YOU WON'T GET SHOT.

TELL THEM THAT JESSE JAMES WAS HERE.
JESSE JAMES IS ONE OF THE MOST FAMOUS OF THESE OUTLAWS. FROM 1866 TO 1882, JAMES AND HIS GANG ROBBED TRAINS AND BANKS ACROSS THE MIDWEST. THEY WERE A VIOLENT BUNCH THAT DIDN'T THINK TWICE ABOUT SHOOTING AND KILLING ANYONE WHO GOT IN THEIR WAY.

NO LAWMAN WAS EVER ABLE TO CAPTURE OR KILL JESSE JAMES. BUT IN 1882, ONE OF HIS OWN MEN, ROBERT FORD, SHOT AND KILLED JAMES TO GET A $10,000 REWARD.
NO MORE TAKING ORDERS. AND THAT $10,000 IS ALL MINE.

I AIN'T TAKING ANY MORE OF THIS FROM YOU.

HENRY MCCARTY STARTED HIS LIFE OF CRIME AT AN EARLY AGE. HE WAS IN TROUBLE WITH THE LAW BY AGE 15. IN 1877, AT AGE 17, HE SHOT AND KILLED A MAN WHO HAD BEEN BULLYING HIM. THIS STARTED A LIFE ON THE RUN FOR THE OUTLAW WHO LATER BECAME KNOWN AS BILLY THE KID.

THE KID SPENT THE NEXT FOUR YEARS STEALING HORSES AND WORKING AS **A GUN FOR HIRE** IN NEW MEXICO. DURING HIS LIFE OF CRIME, HE WAS CAPTURED MANY TIMES. BUT EACH TIME, HE FOUND A WAY TO ESCAPE.

I'VE GOT YOU THIS TIME, BILLY. THERE'S NO WAY OUT.

IN 1881, BILLY WAS CAUGHT AND JAILED BY PAT GARRETT, A FORMER FRIEND WHO HAD BECOME A **SHERIFF**. BILLY THE KID KILLED TWO GUARDS AND ESCAPED. BUT A FEW MONTHS LATER, GARRETT FOUND HIM AND GUNNED HIM DOWN. AT JUST 21 YEARS OLD, BILLY THE KID HAD BECOME ONE OF THE MOST FAMOUS OUTLAWS OF THE WEST.

THERE WERE PLENTY OF OTHER OUTLAWS, AS WELL. MANY PEOPLE SAW THE OUTLAWS AS HEROES, FIGHTING BACK AGAINST THE RICH. OUTLAW STORIES FILLED NEWSPAPERS ACROSS THE NATION. BOOKS WERE WRITTEN ABOUT THEIR MANY ADVENTURES. BUT MOST OF THE OUTLAWS WERE JUST COLD-BLOODED KILLERS. THEY WANTED TO BECOME RICH THEMSELVES.

SAYS HERE THAT THE BANDITS MADE OFF WITH MORE THAN $600 FROM THAT BANK IN EL PASO.
GOOD FOR THEM. THE BANKS WON'T MISS IT. THEY'VE GOT PLENTY MORE.
HOW CAN YOU SAY THAT? STEALIN'S NEVER RIGHT!

LEGENDARY LAWMEN

AS OUR SHERIFF, IT WILL BE YOUR JOB TO UPHOLD THE LAW. YOU'RE GOING TO PROTECT US.
AND YOU'LL PAY ME.

OUTLAWS MADE LIFE HARD ON BANKS, RANCHES, AND OTHER BUSINESSES. THE GOVERNMENT USED U.S. MARSHALS TO KEEP THE PEACE. SOME TOWNS HIRED SHERIFFS TO DO THE JOB. THESE LAWMEN HAD TO BE AS TOUGH AS THEIR ENEMIES. MANY HAD ALSO BEEN IN TROUBLE WITH THE LAW IN THE PAST.

THE LAWMEN WERE GIVEN GREAT FREEDOM. FEW QUESTIONS WERE ASKED ABOUT HOW THEY DID THEIR JOBS. THEY MIGHT SHOOT A CRIMINAL IN THE STREET OR BRING HIM TO BE JAILED AND TRIED. AS LONG AS THEY GOT RID OF THE OUTLAWS, THE TOWNS THAT HIRED THEM WERE HAPPY.
HE WON'T BE CAUSING US ANY MORE TROUBLE.

THERE WAS NO GREATER LAWMAN THAN "WILD BILL" HICKOK. HICKOK SERVED AS A FRONTIER SCOUT AND A **MARSHAL** IN KANSAS. HE WAS KNOWN FOR HIS QUICK AND DEADLY SHOT.

WYATT EARP WAS THE MOST FAMOUS OF THE WESTERN LAWMEN. AS PART OF THE GROUP CALLED THE "PEACE COMMISSIONERS," HE PROTECTED DODGE CITY, KANSAS. IN 1881, HE TOOK PART IN A FAMOUS GUNFIGHT. EARP, HIS BROTHERS, AND DOC HOLLIDAY BATTLED A GROUP OF **RANCHERS** AT THE O.K. CORRAL IN TOMBSTONE, ARIZONA. SOME PEOPLE SAY EARP WAS FIGHTING OFF OUTLAWS. OTHERS SAY IT WAS JUST AN ARGUMENT BETWEEN TWO ENEMY GROUPS. EARP SURVIVED THE BATTLE AND BECAME A **LEGEND**.

WOMEN OF THE WEST

WOMEN MADE THEIR MARK ON THE WEST, AS WELL. MANY WOMEN DID THEIR PART BY RAISING THEIR FAMILIES, WORKING ON THEIR FARMS, AND HELPING IN THEIR COMMUNITIES. THE WORK WAS NOT EXCITING, BUT IT WAS JUST AS IMPORTANT AS MEN'S WORK.
WHEN I FINISH WITH THESE PANTS, WE WILL GO TO CHECK IN ON MR. JOHNSTON.

BUT SOME WOMEN MADE A NAME FOR THEMSELVES IN OTHER WAYS. ANNIE OAKLEY WAS ONE OF THE BEST SHOTS IN THE WEST. SHE OFTEN SHOWED OFF HER TALENT IN SHOWS OR CONTESTS. SHE WOULD HAVE SOMEONE THROW A PLAYING CARD IN THE AIR. OAKLEY WOULD THEN SHOOT IT FULL OF HOLES BEFORE IT HIT THE GROUND.
THAT'S WHY THEY CALL HER LITTLE SURE SHOT!

CALAMITY JANE TRAVELED THE WEST IN SEARCH OF ADVENTURE. SHE DRESSED AND ACTED LIKE A MAN, SO SHE WAS EVEN ABLE TO PASS AS A SOLDIER FOR A SHORT TIME. LATER IN LIFE, SHE TOOK PART IN A TRAVELING SHOW, DOING HORSE-RIDING AND SHOOTING TRICKS.

IT IS NOT THE THINGS YOU HAVE THAT MAKE YOU HAPPY. IT IS LOVE AND KINDNESS AND HELPING EACH OTHER AND JUST PLAIN BEING GOOD.※

WOMEN WRITERS HAVE GIVEN US SOME OF THE GREATEST STORIES ABOUT THE WEST. LAURA INGALLS WILDER'S "LITTLE HOUSE" BOOKS TELL THE STORY OF A FRONTIER FAMILY THROUGH THE EYES OF A CHILD.

CONNECTING EAST AND WEST

PONY EXPRESS
WANTED
HOW DO THEY DO IT?

EVEN AFTER MANY TOWNS HAD BEEN BUILT IN THE WEST, IT WAS STILL A VERY DIFFERENT PLACE FROM THE EAST. LONG DISTANCES KEPT THE TWO AREAS SEPARATE FROM EACH OTHER. THE ONLY WAY TO GET A MESSAGE ACROSS THE COUNTRY WAS BY MAIL. BUT THIS WAS VERY SLOW. IN 1860, A PRIVATE MAIL SERVICE CALLED THE PONY EXPRESS WAS FORMED. IT CUT MAIL DELIVERY TIME IN HALF.

ST. JOSEPH
BE CAREFUL. YOU'RE CARRYING A LETTER THAT'S IMPORTANT TO ME.
IT WILL BE IN CALIFORNIA IN TEN DAYS, SAFE AND SOUND.

WHILE U.S. MAIL WAS CARRIED BY SLOW STAGECOACHES, THE PONY EXPRESS HIRED YOUNG, DARING MEN TO CARRY THEIR PACKAGES. THEY RODE AT FULL SPEED, STOPPING AT STATIONS EVERY TEN TO 15 MILES (16.09 TO 24.13 KMS). THEY SWITCHED HORSES OFTEN ON THE 1,120 MILE (1,800 KM) TRIP.

THEY RODE DAY AND NIGHT, FACING OUTLAW ATTACKS, CONFLICTS WITH NATIVE AMERICANS, AND OTHER DANGERS. BUT FOR THEIR HARD WORK, THEY WERE PAID $100 EACH MONTH—A VERY GOOD AMOUNT OF MONEY.

BUT THE PONY EXPRESS WOULD NOT LAST LONG. IN 1861, TELEGRAPH LINES REACHED ACROSS THE COUNTRY. THE TELEGRAPH LET PEOPLE SEND MESSAGES FROM COAST TO COAST IN JUST SECONDS. THERE WAS SOON LITTLE NEED FOR THE RIDERS OF THE PONY EXPRESS.

I'VE SENT THEM YOUR COMPLETE ORDER. IS THERE ANYTHING ELSE THAT YOU'D LIKE TO ADD?
NO, THAT WILL BE FINE.

ARE WE THERE YET?
GETTING MESSAGES ACROSS THE COUNTRY WAS HARD. MOVING PEOPLE AND GOODS WAS EVEN HARDER. FOR MANY YEARS, A STAGECOACH WAS THE ONLY WAY TO MAKE THE TRIP. THE TRIP ACROSS THE COUNTRY TOOK MONTHS AND WAS VERY UNCOMFORTABLE.
NOT YET, MY DEAR. WE WON'T BE THERE FOR A LONG, LONG TIME.

BUT THAT STARTED TO CHANGE WHEN THE PACIFIC RAILROAD ACT WAS PASSED IN 1862. IT CALLED FOR TWO COMPANIES TO BEGIN BUILDING RAILROADS. A TEAM OF CHINESE WORKERS STARTED IN SAN FRANCISCO AND MOVED TOWARD THE EAST. A TEAM OF IRISH WORKERS STARTED IN OMAHA AND WORKED WEST.
MAKE SURE THAT THOSE CROSS-TIES ARE STRAIGHT.

THIS GOLDEN SPIKE MARKS THE END OF OUR WORK. BUT IT ALSO MARKS THE BEGINNING OF A NEW AGE!

IT WAS A HUGE JOB THAT TOOK MANY YEARS TO FINISH. IN THE WINTER OF 1868 AND 1869, MORE THAN 25,000 MEN WORKED ON THE TRACKS. FINALLY, ON MAY 10, 1869, THE TEAMS MET UP IN PROMONTORY, UTAH. THEY HAMMERED A GOLDEN SPIKE INTO THE LAST RAILROAD TIE.

TRAVEL TO AND FROM THE WEST SOON BECAME SAFE, FAST, AND COMFORTABLE. CROPS, ANIMALS, AND OTHER GOODS WERE MOVED MORE EASILY, TOO. THIS ALLOWED THE WEST TO GROW QUICKLY. BY THE LATE 1800S, THE EAST AND THE WEST WERE SEPARATE NO MORE. THEY WERE PART OF ONE, UNITED NATION.

TIMELINE

1492 — COLUMBUS ARRIVES IN THE AMERICAS; EUROPEANS AND NATIVE AMERICANS MAKE THEIR FIRST CONTACT.

1689 — THE FRENCH AND INDIAN WARS BEGIN; THE BRITISH WIN CONTROL OVER THE CONTINENT BUT REMAIN IN CONFLICT WITH THE INDIANS.

1815 — THE TREATY OF GHENT ENDS THE WAR OF 1812 BETWEEN THE UNITED STATES AND BRITAIN.

1830 — U.S. PRESIDENT ANDREW JACKSON SIGNS THE INDIAN REMOVAL ACT, REQUIRING THAT ALL NATIVE AMERICANS BE MOVED WEST OF THE MISSISSIPPI RIVER.

1838 — THE U.S. MILITARY REMOVES SOME 15,000 CHEROKEE FROM THEIR HOMES IN GEORGIA AND MARCHES THEM TO OKLAHOMA; THE DEADLY TRIP COMES TO BE KNOWN AS THE "TRAIL OF TEARS."

1848 — GOLD IS DISCOVERED IN CALIFORNIA, LEADING TO THE CALIFORNIA GOLD RUSH THE FOLLOWING YEAR.

1860 — THE PONY EXPRESS IS CREATED; THE SERVICE USES DARING YOUNG RIDERS

TO CARRY MAIL ACROSS THE COUNTRY.

1862 – THE HOMESTEAD ACT IS SIGNED, PROMISING LAND TO FAMILIES WILLING TO MOVE WEST; MORE THAN 600,000 SETTLERS ARE DRAWN TO THE WEST OVER THE NEXT 40 YEARS.

1869 – THE LAST SPIKE IS DRIVEN INTO THE TRANSCONTINENTAL RAILROAD, CONNECTING THE EAST AND WEST OF THE UNITED STATES.

1876 – ARMSTRONG CUSTER IS DEFEATED BY THE SIOUX AND CHEYENNE IN "CUSTER'S LAST STAND," ONE OF THE WORST MILITARY DEFEATS IN U.S. HISTORY.

1881 – "PEACE COMMISSIONERS" LED BY WYATT EARP DEFEAT RANCHERS IN THE FAMOUS GUNFIGHT AT THE O.K. CORRAL IN TOMBSTONE, ARIZONA.

1932 – LAURA INGALLS WILDER PUBLISHES *LITTLE HOUSE IN THE BIG WOODS*, THE FIRST OF HER BOOKS ABOUT GROWING UP ON THE FRONTIER.

GLOSSARY

BEQUEATH GIVE OVER TO

BOOMTOWN A TOWN THAT QUICKLY SPRUNG UP AFTER GOLD WAS DISCOVERED IN THE WEST

COLONIST A PERSON LIVING IN A NEWLY SETTLED AREA THAT IS UNDER THE CONTROL OF ANOTHER COUNTRY'S GOVERNMENT

FRONTIER THE EDGES OF SETTLED OR DEVELOPED LANDS

GENERAL A HIGH RANKING OFFICER

GUN FOR HIRE WILLING TO FIGHT AND/OR KILL FOR MONEY

LEGEND A PERSON WHO IS REMEMBERED IN STORIES

MARSHAL AN OFFICER OF THE U.S. GOVERNMENT THAT HELPS TO KEEP THE PEACE

MASSACRE THE ACT OF KILLING A NUMBER OF HELPLESS PEOPLE

MILITARY THE ARMED FORCES (SUCH AS THE ARMY AND NAVY) OF A NATION

MORMONS FOLLOWERS OF A RELIGION FOUNDED IN 1830 BY JOSEPH SMITH, JR.

NATIVE AMERICAN ANY OF THE GROUPS OF PEOPLES WHO LIVED IN THE AMERICAS BEFORE THE ARRIVAL OF EUROPEANS, SOMETIMES CALLED INDIANS

RANCHER A PERSON WHO RAISES ANIMALS ON A RANCH

RESISTANCE THE ACT OF FIGHTING AGAINST OR OPPOSING SOMETHING

SETTLER A PERSON THAT MOVES INTO A NEW AREA OR REGION

SHERIFF AN OFFICIAL WHO ENFORCES THE LAW IN A CITY, TOWN, OR COUNTY

SODDIES HOUSES MADE OUT OF BRICKS OF SOIL

SUBSISTENCE THE STATE OF LIVING ON VERY LITTLE

UNITED BROUGHT TOGETHER AS ONE

INDEX

WEBFINDER

HTTP://WWW.AMERICANWEST.COM/

HTTP://WWW.NANATIONS.COM/

HTTP://PBSKIDS.ORG/WAYBACK/GOLDRUSH/INDEX.HTML

HTTP://WWW.EYEWITNESSTOHISTORY.COM/OWFRM.HTM

HTTP://WWW.PBS.ORG/WGBH/AMEX/TCRR/